# DOMINICAN REPUBLIC

## PHOTOGRAPHED BY MICHAEL FRIEDEL

TEXT BY MARION FRIEDEL
TRANSLATED BY ANGUS MC GEOCH

EDITION MM

ntilles, West Indies, Caribbean - three names for one and the same region, the arc of islands which stretches around the Caribbean Sea from North to South America. La Española, Hispaniola, Haiti, Dominican republic. "The most beautiful land that ever a human eye has gazed upon," as the great seafarer Christopher Columbus rapturously described the island, which he named "La Española" in honour of Spain. In the course of time this became Hispaniola - Little Spain - one of the four names associated with the second largest island in the Antilles, which since 1844 has been divided into two nations, Haiti and the Dominican Republic.

Welcome to paradise! Long beaches, endless sea, luxuriant vegetation. A pyrotechnic display of colour. Air like velvet. Eternal sunshine. Friendly faces. This is your holiday destination: the Dominican Republic, where tourism has boomed since the late 1980s.

The authors, internationally known photographer Michael Friedel and his journalist wife Marion, have been travelling round the Caribbean islands since the 1970s. In their 1981 book of photographs: "Islands of the Caribbean - Columbus, Cuba, Carnival" - not much space was devoted to the Dominican Republic as a holiday destination among the 31 island communities of the Caribbean. But today over two million tourists come here every year, and so the authors set off to rediscover this part of the island of Hispaniola. Through the green valleys, across deserts and over mountains, along the coast to the vast hotel complexes, deserted bays, romantic beaches - sometimes in a "four-by-four" and sometimes looking out of a helicopter.

It was in the mid-1980s that Oscar Nausch first came to the Dominican Republic; and he fell in love with the country and its people. He had at last found what he had always been searching for: a tropical climate with sunshine all year round, a place where winter is unknown; tropical rain-forests, broad savannah and deserts, palm-fringed beaches, mountain pastures basking in a January sun, mangrove swamps, cliff-girt coasts, archipelagos with dozens of small islands, sand-dunes, mountain streams and waterfalls, endless plantations of sugar-cane and coconuts, Spanish-colonial country houses, 16th century castles and walled towns, colourful Caribbean cottages, fishing-boats and sailing-yachts, friendly and uninhibited people. Oscar works hard in his paradise. The Friedels are among the many who have made good use of his profound knowledge of the country's

Michael Friedel
Oskar Nausch

towns, villages and landscapes. His one-man business, 'Luna Caribe' organises locations-shoots for film and television companies and fashion photographers. As a man who knows the place like the back of his hand, he has written the extensive information section of this book, and on page 86 he passes on his own special travel experiences to the reader. Because people who come here on 'all-inclusive' holidays shouldn't spend all the time in their hotel or resort complex; instead they should endeavour to get to know this fascinating country and its population. Oscar will point you towards the many possibilities that can often be missing from an 'all-inclusive' package, even if it is in the luxury class. You will only discover all the things this beautiful country has to offer the enterprising visitor if, guided by your curiosity, you let yourself be tempted into making expeditions and tours around the island republic.

# NOTES ON THE ILLUSTRATION

PUNTA CANO on SAMANÁ is a small, palm-fringed bay sheltered by low hills. It can only be reached on foot or by boat. During the day you can have the beach to yourself but in the evening fishermen come and pull their boats up on the sand. In the Dominican Republic, with more than 1500 km (900 miles) of coastline, deserted beaches are not rare. (pages 8-9)

CAYO LEVANTADO, also known as "Bacardi Island", is the main excursion point in the bay of Samaná. Though scarcely 2km long and 500m wide (1.2 by 0.3 miles) hundreds of day-trippers bask in the romantic atmosphere of the island's three beaches. Only in the early morning and evening can the guests at the small but luxurious Cayo Levantado Beach Hotel lay exclusive claim to the overcrowded island. (pages 10-11)

PUNTA BONITA on SAMANÁ at 7 in the morning, shortly after sunrise. Sheer solitude is yours on the wild and almost deserted white sand beach over 20km (12 miles) long, with an unbroken border of palm forest. A protecting reef tames the power of the waves and makes for safe bathing. In small hotels near the beach independent travellers will find peace and seclusion. (Pages 12-13)

The ISLA SAONA, an island 117 sq km (45 sq miles) in area, is part of the Parque Nacional del Este" nature reserve. Every day thousands of visitors come on organized day-trips to spend a few hours on the remote beaches of this untouched island. For most of the holidaymakers at the big hotel complexes this expedition is a rare encounter with the natural beauty of the Dominican republic. (pages 14-15)

The coast of BARAHONA. Despite the tourist boom the republic still ranks among the poor countries on earth. "Mio Rancho" is the name proudly given to this log cabin built from driftwood, without water or electricity, but with a sea view.  Once home to a family of nine, the shack is now for sale. The rural population is irresistibly drawn to the towns, in the belief that they will find work and thus a future there. (pages 16-17)

The variety of the island's landscape delighted Columbus 500 years ago. In the south, near PUNTA CANA, the Caribbean king palms rise from the green savanna to a height of 30m (98 ft). The coconut palms, being resistant to salt water, border the PUNTA BONITA and many other beaches. The largest forests of coconut palms are found on the Samaná peninsula. Words by Marion Friedel. (Pages 18-21)

In the south-west of the country, near BARAHONA, we met "Joselyn" bathing in the Rio Baoruco. Tourists rarely visit this area, and the local people enjoy being photographed. The wild landscape of this region is being opened up with a new highway running along the country's most beautiful coast as far as PEDERNALES on the border with Haiti. Words by Marion Friedel. (Pages 22-23)

The DOMINICUS club is one large hotel complex on the mile-long beach near BAYAHIBE on the east end of the island. The club is under Italian management and offers "all-inclusive" sports and entertainment virtually round the clock. From the nearby fishing-village of BAYAHIBE speed-boats and catamarans take organized groups on day excursions to the offshore island, ISLA SAONA.(pages 26-27)

# NOTES ON THE ILLUSTRATION

A unique natural drama is played out annually from December to February in the BAY OF SAMANÁ. Hundreds of hump-backed whales come here to mate and to calve. The growing number of tourists annoys these sensitive giants and they are withdrawing more and more to the protected Silverbanks area. The little bay below the Hotel Cayacoa in Samaná Town is mainly visited by Dominican guests. (pages 60-61)

On the way up to the PICO DUARTE, at 3175m (10,414ft) the highest mountain in the Caribbean. In the green mountain landscape near JARABACOA at an altitude of 675m (2.200ft) the steamy tropical climate is suddenly left behind. "The air is like April in Castile," Christoph Columbus once wrote in his ship's logbook. The average daytime temperature is only 26∞ C. (76∞ F) Wealthy Dominicans have their summer homes here. (pages 62-63)

Mountain rivers and waterfalls are a paradise for white-water enthusiasts. The 55m (180ft) high EL LIMON waterfall in SAMANÁ flows all year round. Cascading - abseiling down the waterfall - is the new sport run by a mountain guide from the Austrian Tirol. On the river YAQUE DEL NORTE near JARABACOA rafting trips set off daily. Anyone aged over 14 can take part in all these activities without previous experience. (pages 64-65)

The east of the country, along the CORDILLERA ORIENTAL, is an expanse of wide, grassy savannas, dotted with king-palms, and supporting large cattle-ranches. The government is making efforts to develop agriculture further. Over two million tourists visit the republic every year. In future all their food will be grown locally.
(pages 66-67)

In the midst of sugar-cane fields on the main road from PUERTO PLATA to SANTIAGO stands the impressive "Amistad" sugar mill. For 3 months of the year work goes on 24 hours a day in a total of 16 sugar factories around the country. Conditions are so wretched that despite high unemployment Haitians have to be "imported". The pay for a tonne of sugarcane is only a few pesos, enough to buy a packet of cigarettes. (pages 68-69)

In the period around 27 February, the anniversary of independence from Haiti in 1844, the carnival is held in SANTO DOMINGO. On the waterfront Avenida de George Washington, also known as the Malecón, or sea-wall, a procession of 30,000 people parades past half a million spectators. The atmosphere is heightened by the best Merengue bands on big bandstands. "Baile en la calle de noche/ baile en la calle de día (Dance in the streets

by night/ dance in the streets by day...)". The "Diablos Cojuelos", or "Limping Devils" from LA VEGA and SANTO DOMINGO are the most famous carnival masks. Groups of various sizes in matching costumes parade through the streets. They swing inflated bladders of pigs or cows, called "vejigas", and bring them down with considerable force on the heads the "sinful" spectators.
(pages 70-73)

SANTO DOMINGO, "la única ciudad gótica de America" (the only Gothic city in the Americas), was founded in 1496 by Bartolomeo Columbus, the brother of the explorer, as the first city in the new world. A visit to the Old City and the fortified palace ALCÁZAR DE COLON, built in 1510-14 and renovated in 1957, is a must for everyone including pupils of the Escuela Republica del Ecuador. (pages 74-75)

# NOTES ON THE ILLUSTRATION

One of over 30 slum districts in the capital, SANTO DOMINGO, where over 2 1/2 million people are crammed into an area of just 162 sq. km (63 sq. miles). The overwhelming majority live miserably in appalling conditions. Torrential rainfall damages the houses made of wood and junk materials. The paint for the colourful housefronts is regularly donated by the political parties before the presidential elections, every four years. (pages 76-77)

Cultural evidence of the aboriginal population, the TAINOS, is chiefly to be found in museums. Huge sums were spent on the renovation of the "Zona Colonial" in the run-up to the quincentenary of Columbus. The "Torre del Homenaje", built 1502-1507, was a torture tower, prison and place of execution for Indians, rebels and heretics. From 1503 to 1924 it served as the standard-bearer for the 7 nations which successively occupied Santo Domingo. (pages 78-79)

"LAS CARITAS" - the cave of the little faces - in the SIERRA DE NEIBA on the salt lake LAGO ENRIQUILLO, is 40m (131ft) below sea-level and the lowest point in the Caribbean. The rock drawings are more than 400 years old and bear witness to the last great rebellion of the Taino Indians, led by their chieftain Enriquillo, against the Spanish. Within a single generation the Spanish had wiped out nine-tenths of the native islanders. (pages 80-81)

"Among the many vices practised by the Indians, one is especially reprehensible. This is to take dried leaves, which they call TABACCO, set them alight and inhale the smoke..." Thus wrote the outraged Oviedo in his "Historica General" of 1535. This vice has conquered the world. Cigarette manufacture in the town of Santiago. Indian clay sculpture in the Museo del Hombre in Santo Domingo. (pages 82-83)

"No hay problemas - no problem." A smile gets you over any language barrier. In the country, far from the tourist centres, foreign visitors are a rarity and cause quite a sensation. The Dominicans welcome some variety in their daily life and are friendly to strangers. With an easy-going, humorous approach and an interest in their problems, you will soon make friends. (pages 84-85)

Large hotel chains, mainly Spanish-owned, have added to the growth of the tourist centres around the three international airports of Puerto Plata, Punta Cana and Santo Domingo. Oskar Nausch, who has known the island for many years, urges you to venture beyond the tourist centres to discover this fascinating country and its people. (pages 86-89)

The creative team of Marion and Michael Friedel, the writer and the photographer, travelled intensively throughout the Dominican Republic on motoconchos, in all-terrain vehicles, by minibus and helicopter, capturing it anew in words and pictures. Since their first visit in the early 1980s, much had changed, especially in tourism.
The Michael Friedel Workshop. (pages 90-91)

On the last pages:
GENERAL INFORMATION
USEFUL TIPS
CLIMATIC TABLES
BOOKS OF TRAVEL AND EXPLORATION
MAP OF THE COUNTRY
OTHER BOOKS BY MICHAEL FRIEDEL
(pages 92-96)

33

49

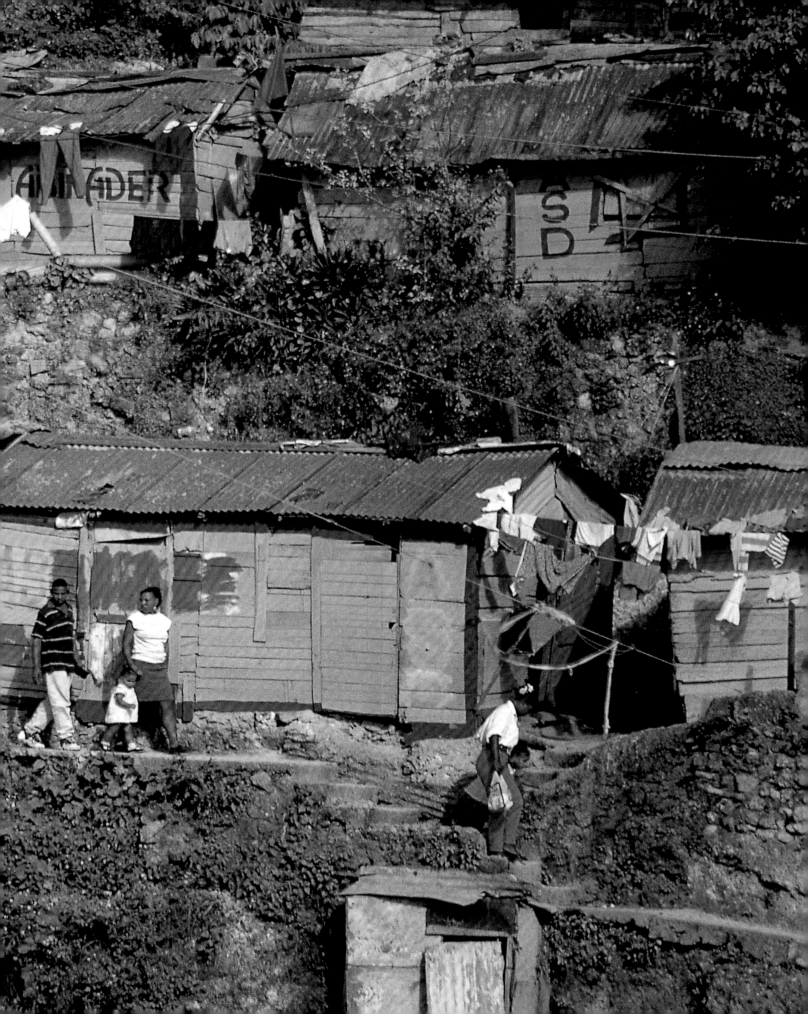

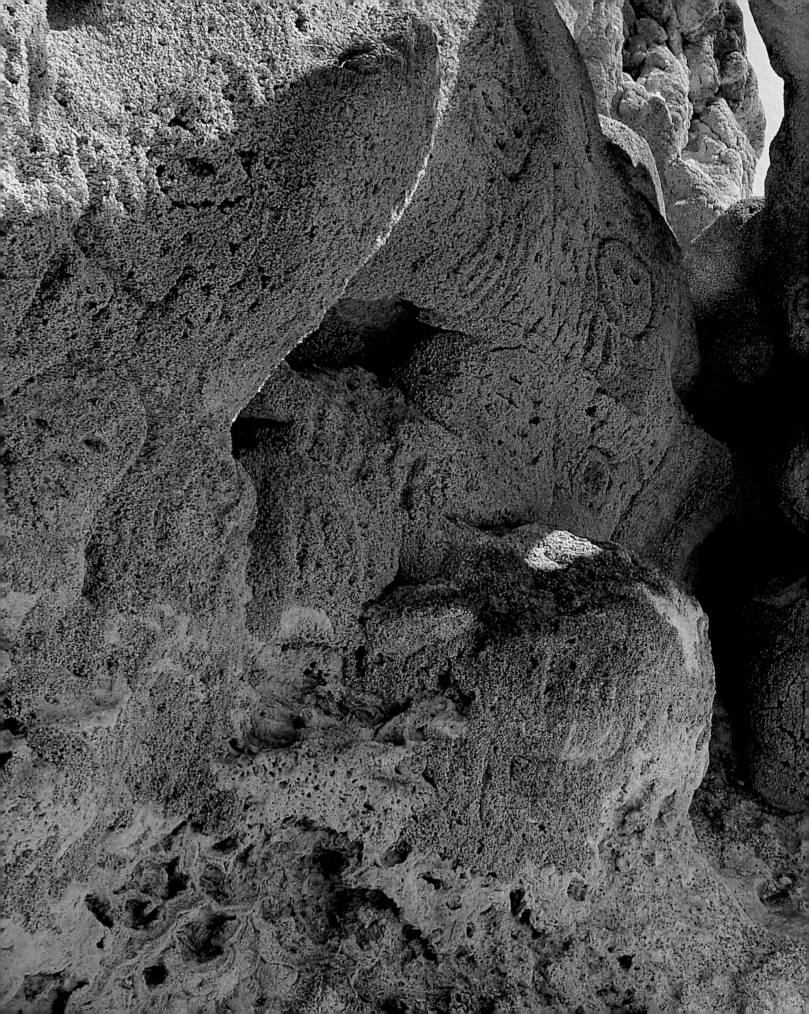

Restaurant Matilde

Bar Las Terrenas - Samaná

Puerto Plata

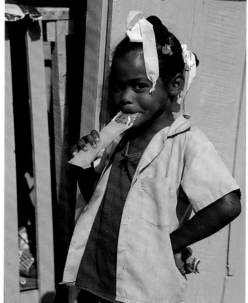

Río San Juan

Colmado - grocery store

Restaurant - Sanchez

Baoruco - Barahona

Joselyne - Rio Bauruco

Higuey - La Altagracia

Enriquillo - Barahona

Carmen - Puerto Plata

84

Ironmonger - Boca Cachon

Musician- Merengue

Jarabacao - La Vega

Oviedo - Pedernales

Las Terrenas - Samaná

Paraiso - Barahona

San Rafael - Barahona

San Pedro de Macoris

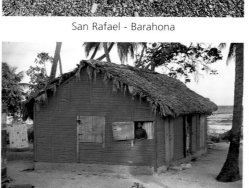

La Cienaga - Barahona

Cockfighting - Baoruco

Luperon - Puerto Plata

Maria - motorway services

# HOTELS

Altos de Savon

Club Dominicus - Bayahibe

Aligio - Las Terrenas

Casa Bonita - Baoruco

Carribean Village - Bavaro

Sea Breeze Hotel - Sosua

Bavaro Beach Resort - Punta Cana

Cayo Levantado - Samaná

Cabarete - Beach

Hamaca Beach - Boca Chica

Juan Dolio - Beach

Playa Dorada  Beach and its hotel complex. In the background Puerto Plata and Mount Isabel de Torres.

Gran Ventana - Playa Dorada

Campo da golf - Playa Dorada

Caribbean Village - Playa Grande

Punta Cana - Beaches

Playa Dorada Hotel - Playa Dorada

Flamenco - Playa Dorada

Paradise - Playa Dorada

Bahia Principe - Playa Grande

## FLIGHTS

From Europe with AIR FRANCE, ALITALIA, BELAIR, BRITANNIA, THOMAS COOK, HAPAG LLOYD, IBERIA, LAUDA AIR, LTU, MARTINAIR, TAP. From the USA with AMERICAN AIRLINES, AMERICAN EAGLE, to the 4 international airports of the Dominican Republic: Puerto Plata, Punta Cana, Santo Domingo, La Romana.

## HOTELS

The **range of hotels** is very wide. Most of the hotel-complexes are by a beach and operate on the **all-inclusive** system. The independent traveller can choose between a luxury hotel (from US$150.-), through small **private hotels** (around US$50), which have taken up the challenge of all-inclusive mass-tourism, and **guesthouses** (from US$15.-) down to **hoteles familiares** (from US$3.-). For people who want to stay longer, a good idea is an **aparthotel** with a cooking area and refrigerator. Caution is needed on the outskirts of towns. Here you will find the **"cabanas"**, often with the word **"turisticas"** added. These establishments are intended more for visits by the hour. The astonished tourist will find the TV programme is limited to porno films and after 4 hours he will be thrown out on the street again.

## ARRIVAL AND CUSTOMS

For entry you need a **passport** valid for at least 3 months ahead and a **Tourist Card** costing US$10.-. This is a kind of diplomatic revenge exacted on citizens of all those states which require Dominicans to obtain an entry visa. Anyone wishing to stay longer than 3 months can get their tourist visa extended without any problem by the immigration authorities in Santo Domingo, in return for a small fee. The **customs** leave the tourist visitors pretty much alone. If you are bringing in electrical goods such as a TV set or computer, you sometimes have to leave a deposit, which is returned when you take the item out of the country. Importing or purchasing **narcotics** is most strongly discouraged. The penalties are draconian and the conditions in law-courts and prisons appalling. Importing fruit, plants and cooked meat (sausages etc) is banned, as in the USA. Diseases affecting animals and plants have already caused great damage to the country's agriculture.

## CLOTHING AND EQUPMENT

We recommend light, comfortable summer clothing, with long trousers as protection against the mosquitoes which are active at dusk, and a hat or cap to prevent sunstroke. As regards dress code, the Dominicans are rather conservative. In churches and official buildings such as the presidential palace or the palace of justice, no-one is admitted wearing shorts or a miniskirt. Nude or topless bathing is frowned on. On the other hand foreigners are allowed to get away with a lot.

## CURRENCY

The national currency is the peso (= 100 centavos). Internationally it is linked to the US dollar. Currently there is no black market to speak of. Only change money in banks and bureaux de change, as money-changers on the street will cheat you. US dollar travellers cheques are the safest means of payment. The major credit-cards are accepted in most hotels. You can get cash, but only pesos, with credit-cards: Visa, Eurocard and Mastercard, for example in the Banco Popular. American Express is handled by the Banco de Progreso.

**Caution!!!** The symbol **$** can stand for pesos as well as for US dollars!

## INTER-ISLAND CONNECTIONS

The best way to Puerto Rico is by one of the dozen flights each day. All other islands are best reached by flying first to Miami. To Haiti there are regular flights from Santo Domingo in small planes, e.g. with Air Santo Domingo. But it is cheaper to go by bus.

## TELEVISION, PRESS AND BOOKS

There are 9 Dominican channels and over 50 international channels, mainly from the USA, received via satellite. There are several dozen radio stations and on UHF alone there are five morning and two afternoon news programmes. Foreign newspapers and books are generally only found in hotels.

## ELECTRICITY

110 volt, American socket system.

## MEDICINE

**Innoculations** are not required for entry to the Dom. Rep. Anti-malaria precautions are only recommended for those also visiting neighbouring Haiti. All the hotels provide **doctors** who speak English. If you have to be hospitalized avoid the dreadful **state hospitals** and go to one of the significantly cleaner and technically better equipped private clinics. Most normal medications can be bought without a prescription at a **"farmacia."** Important medication that you require personally should be brought with you in sufficient quantity.

## CAR RENTAL, TAXIS AND AIRCRAFT

Due to the high import duty on road vehicles **renting a car** is relatively expensive. There are international firms (Budget, Hertz, Thrifty), national ones (Nelly, National) and also local car-rental firms. For the northern European, getting involved in Dominican traffic requires a radical mental adjustment. People here do not drive in the way the regulations prescribe, but in whatever way happens to suit them. For instance, even when the lights are green, you should still expect cars to come at you from right and left, either because the lights are not working, or because the other driver is in a hurry or is simply drunk. The typical British habit of playing it by the book in traffic, is wholly inappropriate. You are well advised to give way to large trucks without question, and the same goes for pretty female motorists. Driving at night should be avoided as far as possible, since not all vehicles carry lights; and pedestrians, donkeys etc. wander about on the roadway. There is virtually no such thing as street lighting. Traffic policemen are recognizable by their white plastic tropical topees. If you are stopped by one, he will first shake you warmly by the hand, expecting a small tip, a road-toll, so to speak. Anyone brave enough to hire a **motor-cycle** should stay as far from busy roads as possible. If you prefer to be driven by someone else, you can travel by **bus** without difficulty to the remotest corners of the country.

There are large bus companies offering air-conditioning, reservable seats and bus-stops (Metro Tours, Caribe Tours) and a multitude of driver-cooperatives, which cover practically every route in the country - mostly with buses called **"guaguas"**, which are jam-packed. It is true you are cramped, the music is deafening and live hens and bunches of bananas are also being carried, yet the natural warmth and openness of your Dominican fellow-passengers makes these minor discomforts well worth putting up with. You will learn more about the country and its people in half an hour than from months of lying beside the hotel pool.When the buses can go no further, the passengers get into the back of a **pickup**. For short journeys and night excursions there are taxis, usually old Chevvies and Dodges from the 1960s and '70s. You should negotiate the fare before you start. Price-lists are also hung up in most hotels. In small towns and villages little 50cc or 70cc mopeds serve as taxis, and are then known as "motoconchos." They are capable of carrying up to 5 adults, alternatively two medium sized pigs and a passenger to hold on to them, or half a dozen sacks of agricultural produce. You can often scarcely believe what you are seeing. The fare depends on the time of day. It goes up after dark and up again at midnight. If you are in a hurry and have a long distance to cover, you can charter a private aircraft. You can choose between half a dozen firms, which all have their offices at Santo Domingo's small Herera airport. Prices go from US$150 per hour's flying time. This way you can quickly get to remote areas. For example, you can fly from Santo Domingo to Samaná in about 45 mins, compared with 5 hours by car. There is also a small airline, Bavaro Sunflight, which connects Santo Domingo with Punta Cana and Puerto Plata.

## CLIMATIC TABLES

| | Jan. | Mar. | May | July | Sept. | Nov. |
|---|---|---|---|---|---|---|
| Mean daytime maximum temperature in °C | 29 | 29 | 30 | 31 | 31 | 30 |
| Mean nighttime minimum temperature in °C | 18 | 19 | 22 | 22 | 22 | 21 |
| Mean daily hours of sunshine | 9 | 9 | 8 | 8 | 8 | 8 |
| Mean days with rain per month | 3 | 7 | 13 | 7 | 12 | 7 |

## FOOD AND DRINK

**Dominican cuisine** is anything but sophisticated. Dominicans eat chiefly to fill their stomachs. The cornerstone of the national diet is the **"Bandera Dominicana"**. At 12 o'clock sharp every Dominican has to have his **"viveres"** - a huge plate of rice and red beans, boiled bananas, a leg of chicken and some salad and vegetables. Sadly, it is easier to get a Chinese, Japanese, Italian or even German meal than to find typical Dominican food. The best Dominican food, costing very little, is served in **"comedores"** throughout the country - from 12 noon, hot from the oven. And with a vast choice of fruit and fruit-juices. A favourite with hard drinkers is coconut milk. It cures a hangover and increases potency. The hangover will have been caused by the good locally brewed **beer** ("Presidente") or the even better **rum**, from one of the three big B's: Barceló, Brugal and Bermúdez. You can choose between brown or white rum. The author's favourite brands are "Barceló Imperial" for drinking neat, and "Barceló Añejo" for mixing. Watch out for rum bottles which have the number 151 on them. That stuff is over 70% proof spirit. Only people who want to get drunk in a hurry should drink it neat. It is really fit for nothing but stripping paint.

## TELEPHONES

In the Dom.Rep. there are several competing telephone companies - Codetel, Orange, Tricom, All American - so the charges are reasonable. You can buy telephone-cards at their offices. Calls from hotels are expensive.

## LANGUAGE

The national language is **Spanish**, but very different from the Castilian language of Spain. **English** is only spoken by the well educated, or by Dominicans who went to the USA and were later deported as illegal immigrants.

## TIME

Four hours behind GMT, or 5 hours behind British Summer Time.

## SPORT AND LEISURE

For **snorkelling** and **scuba-diving** the south coast between Punta Cana and Cabo Rojo is the most suitable. The water of the Caribbean Sea is rather warmer and has a lower swell than the Atlantic Ocean on the north side. Particularly good diving areas are found in La Romana, Bayahibe, Catalina and Cabo Rojo. **Golf** is played in Santo Domingo, Puerto Plata, Punta Cana and Juan Dolio, but above all at the three world-famous courses of the Casa de Campo hotel in La Romana. There are **tennis-courts** in every medium-sized and large hotel complex. **Baseball** is the most popular sport, while football is scarcely known here. Nr 2 in the popularity scale is cock-fighting. If you want to go rambling or **mountain-biking**, you have to head into the mountains; from 1000m (3,300 ft) above sea-level the temperature becomes tolerable.

## SOUVENIRS

Paintings come in by the truckload from Haiti and shell necklaces are imported from the Philippines. **Amber** is found on the island and made into decorative articles. The only place in the world where a sky-blue semi-precious stone called **larimar** is found, is in a mine near Barahona. You can buy the best **cigars** in the world, and good **rum**. Haggling is no disgrace in the Caribbean. In fact it is expected.

## HOLIDAY SEASONS AND RAINY SEASONS

There is no rainy season. The best time for a holiday is between December and the end of April - when the weather is at its driest and coolest. The trade winds almost always blow from the east-north-east, which means the dampest and most fertile regions are those furthest to the north and east of the island. The south-west lies in the lee of the high mountains. Rain showers are a rarity here and the climate is desert-like. If you are "lucky" you may experience a hurricane between June and October. These devastating cyclones are not just dangerous on account of their wind-speeds of up to 400kph (240mph) but more because of the torrential rainfall. The last **hurricane** to hit the island of Hispaniola with full force in 1998, was called "George."

## RELIGION

Most Dominicans are **Catholic**, and the Catholic church has great authority in the country. People are more likely to listen to a bishop than to the often corrupt politicians. There is also a strong presence of the so-called **"evangelical" sects**, such as the Jehovah's Witnesses, the Mormons etc. In the countryside santeria, better known by its Haitian name of **voodoo**, is commonly practised. Most of the "priests" are well-versed in natural medicine. Many Dominicans cannot afford a doctor and go to the **curandero** instead.

## BOOKS OF DISCOVERY AND TRAVEL

Hoetink, Harry: The Dominican People 1850 to 1900, John Hopkins Press 1981
Crassweiler, Robert D.: Trujillo, The Life and Times of a Caribbean Dictator 5. Auflage 1995
Scott, John F.: The Art of the Taino from Dominican Republic, University Presses of Florida 1985
Hazard, Samuel: Santo Domingo Past and Present, with a Glance at Haiti
Harding, Berita: The Land Columbus Loved, Gordon Press 1978
Moya Pons, Frank: The Dominican Republic: A National History Hispaniola Books Corporation 1995
Lowenthal, Abraham F.: Dominican Intervention, John Hopkins Press 1995
Foles, Eric L.: Dominican Republic, Marshall Cavendish 1994
**Oskar Nausch: "Luna Caribe",
e-mail: nausch@tricom.net**

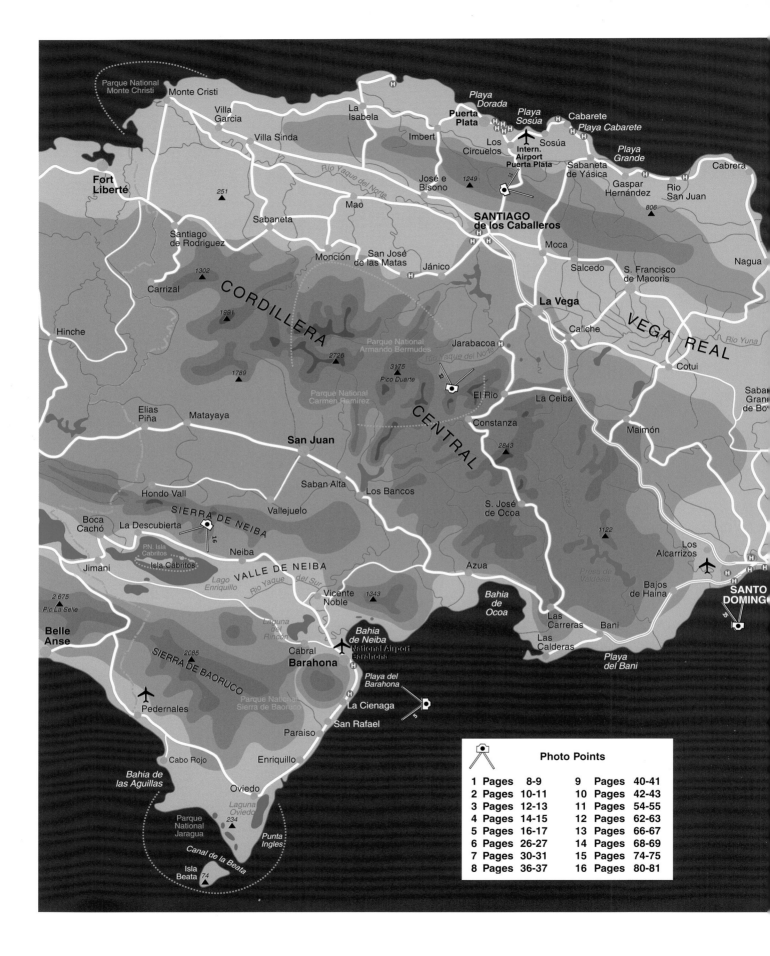

Parque National
Monte Christi

Monte Cristi

Villa
Garcia

La Isabela

Villa Sinda

**Puerta
Plata**

Imbert

*Playa
Dorada*

*Playa
Sosúa*

Cabarete

*Playa Cabarete*

**Fort
Liberté**

251 ▲

Sabaneta

Santiago
de Rodriguez

Los
Circuelos

Sosúa

Intern.
Airport
Puerta Plata

José e
Bisono

1249 ▲

Sabaneta
de Yásica

*Playa
Grande*

Cabrera

Mao

**SANTIAGO
de los Caballeros**

Gaspar
Hernández

Rio
San Juan

806 ▲

Carrizal

1302 ▲

Moncíon

San José
de las Matas

Jánico

Moca

Salcedo

S. Francisco
de Macoris

Nagua

Hinche

1991 ▲

**CORDILLERA**

Parque National
Armando Bermudes

Jarabacoa

**La Vega**

Caliche

**VEGA
REAL**

*Rio Yuna*

2726 ▲

3175 ▲
Pico Duarte

*Rio Yaque del Norte*

El Rio

La Ceiba

Cotui

Saba
Grand
de Bo

Elias
Piña

Matayaya

1789 ▲

Parque National
Carmen Ramirez

**CENTRAL**

Constanza

Boca
Cachó

La Descubierta

**SIERRA DE NEIBA**

16

Neiba

**San Juan**

Saban Alta

Los Bancos

2843 ▲

Maimón

Hondo Vall

Vallejuelo

S. José
de Ocoa

1122 ▲

Los
Alcarrizos

Jimani

PN. Isla
Cabritos

Isla Cabritos

*Lago
Enriquillo*

**VALLE DE NEIBA**

*Rio Yaque del Sur*

Azua

*Presa de
Valdesia*

Bajos
de Haina

**SANTO
DOMINGO**

2 675 ▲
Pic La Selle

*Laguna
del
Rincón*

Vicente
Noble

1343 ▲

*Bahia
de
Ocoa*

Las
Carreras

Bani

**Belle
Anse**

2085 ▲

**SIERRA DE BAORUCO**

Cabral

**Barahona**

*Bahia
de Neiba*

National Airport
Barahona

Las
Calderas

*Playa
del Bani*

Pedernales

Parque National
Sierra de Baoruco

*Playa del
Barahona*

La Cienaga

San Rafael

5

Cabo Rojo

Paraiso

Enriquillo

*Bahia de
las Aguillas*

Oviedo

*Laguna
Oviedo*

234 ▲

Parque
National
Jaragua

*Punta
Ingles*

*Canal de la Beata*

Isla
Beata  74 ▲

---

📷  **Photo Points**

| 1 Pages | 8-9 | 9 Pages | 40-41 |
|---|---|---|---|
| 2 Pages | 10-11 | 10 Pages | 42-43 |
| 3 Pages | 12-13 | 11 Pages | 54-55 |
| 4 Pages | 14-15 | 12 Pages | 62-63 |
| 5 Pages | 16-17 | 13 Pages | 66-67 |
| 6 Pages | 26-27 | 14 Pages | 68-69 |
| 7 Pages | 30-31 | 15 Pages | 74-75 |
| 8 Pages | 36-37 | 16 Pages | 80-81 |

## Océano Atlántico
## Atlantic Ocean

Playa Diamante
Playa Laguna Grande
*Bahía Escocesa*
Punta Bonita
El Portillo
Las Terrena
El Limon
Playa de Rincón
Sanchez
Arroyo Barril
Las Gareras
Playa Blanca
Playa Playuela
Samaná
Intern. Airport Arroyo Barril
Punta Balandra
*Bahia de Samaná*
Cayo Levantado
CUEVA INFIERNO
Sabana del la Mar
Parque Nacional Los Haitises
Miches
Lagunas Redonda y Limon
Playa del Muerto

**CORDILLERA ORIENTAL**

Hato Mayer
El Seibo
696
513
Punta Macao
Playa del Macao
Playa Bavaro
8
Higüey
Cabeza de Toro
Intern. Airport Punta Cana
*Rio Ozama*
*Rio Soco*
*Rio Chavon*
ALTOS DE CHAVON
13
*Rio Yuma*
Punta Cana
San Isidoro
San Pedro de Macoris
Juanillo
Playa Juanillo
La Caleta
Boca Chica
Juan Dolio
**La Romana**
Intern. Airport La Romana
Boca de Yuma
Intern. Airport Santo Domingo
Playa La Sardinia
Bayahibe
*Bahia de Yuma*
Isla Catalina
6
Parque Nacional Del Este
*Canal de la Mona*

## Mar Caribe
## Caribbean Sea

Laguna Los Flamenco
9
Isla Saona
Mano Juan
4

USA
OCÉANO ATLÁNTICO
ATLANTIC OCEAN
GULF OF MEXICO
BAHAMAS
CUBA
HISPANIOLA
MEXICO
HAITI
DOMINICAN REPUBLIC
MAR CARIBE
CARIBBEAN SEA

N

# DOMINICAN REPUBLIC

50 km

30 miles~26 nautical miles

# BOOKS PHOTOGRAPHED BY MICHAEL FRIEDEL

German

English

Italian

French

Japanese

German

English

Italian

French

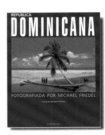
Spanish

German

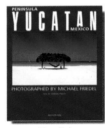
English

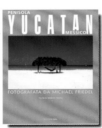
Italian

French

Spanish

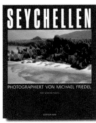
German

English

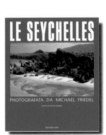
Italian

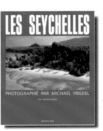
French

German

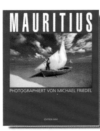
German

1 : 800 000

1 : 800 000

1 : 600 000

**International**: http://www.amazon.com; http://www.barnesandnoble.com; http://www.borders.com
**Germany**: www.amazon.de; www.michael-friedel.de; E-Mail: info@michael-friedel.de
**Austria**: www.freytagberndt.com; **Canada**: www.edipresse.ca
**France**: Vilo Diffusion, 25, rue Ginoux, 75015 Paris, Fax: 01 45 79 97 15; **Switzerland**: www.sbz.ch

**Imprint**
4. English edition; MM-Photodrucke GmbH, 83623 Steingau, Germany; Translated by Angus McGeoch; Concept: Marion & Michael Friedel
Copyright: Marion & Michael Friedel; Photography: Michael Friedel; Titling and design: Stahl Grafikbüro, Munich
Maps: Thomas Braach, Munich; Printing: OrtmannTeam, Ainring, Germany
ISBN 3-929489-18-X Printed in Germany